Parable of the Vineyard

WRITTEN AND ILLUSTRATED BY
Helen Caswell

Abingdon Press
Nashville

Copyright © 1991 by Abingdon Press

All Rights Reserved.

Library of Congress Cataloging-in-Publication Data

Caswell, Helen Rayburn.
  The parable of the vineyard / Helen Caswell.
    p. cm.
  Summary: Jesus compares the kingdom of God to a vineyard in this
parable.
  ISBN 0-687-30021-5 (alk. paper)
  1. Laborers in the vineyard (Parable)—Juvenile literature.
2. Bible stories, English—N.T. Matthew. [1. Laborers in the
vineyard (Parable) 2. Parables. 3. BIble stories—N.T.]
I. Title.
BT378.l3C75   1991
226.8'09505—dc20   90-23228

PRINTED IN SINGAPORE

There once was a man who owned a vineyard.

One morning very early, he went into town to the marketplace, to hire some people to come to his vineyard and pick his grapes, which were very ripe.

He told the people that he would pay each of them a piece of silver for a day's work.

Then all the people went to the vineyard.

After breakfast, some more people came wanting
work to do, so he hired them, too.

In the middle of the day, more people who needed jobs came, and he hired them, too.

Late in the day, a few more people came looking for work, and even though it was late, the owner hired them.

Then evening came.

At quitting time, the workers gathered around the man who owned the vineyard to get their pay.

First came the workers who had started latest in the day. They each received one piece of silver.

Then came the workers who had come at noon.
They each got one piece of silver, too.

Then came the people who had worked all day, since very early in the morning. They each got one piece of silver, too, just as the others had.

"This isn't fair!" they shouted. "We've worked all day long—much longer than these others! We should get more silver than the people who have worked only for an hour or two!"

The owner of the vineyard smiled.

   He said, "Why are you so angry? Did you not get just what I promised you? And was the work so hard? You seemed happy while you were working. And should not these other workers make a living, too?"

Jesus said that the kingdom of God is like a vineyard. People who spend their whole lives working for God should not be angry if those who come late to God receive the same reward. God loves us all the same, whether we are able to do a lot or just a little.